BE WITH

BE WITH
Forrest Gander

WITH PHOTOGRAPHS BY MICHAEL FLOMEN

 A New Directions Book

Manufactured in the United States of America
New Directions Books are printed on acid-free paper
First published as New Directions Paperbook 1408 in 2018

Library of Congress Cataloging-in-Publication Data
Names: Gander, Forrest, 1956– author. | Flomen, Michael, photographer.
Title: Be with / Forrest Gander ; with six photographs by Michael Flomen.
Description: First edition. | New York : New Directions Publishing Corporation, 2018.
Identifiers: LCCN 2018002148 | ISBN 9780811226059 (alk. paper)
Subjects: LCSH: John of the Cross, Saint, 1542–1591—Poetry. | Mothers—Death—Poetry. |
Mexican-American Border Region—Poetry.
Classification: LCC PS3557.A47 A6 2018 | DDC 811/.54—dc23
LC record available at https://lccn.loc.gov/2018002148

10 9 8 7 6 5 4 3

New Directions Books are published for James Laughlin
by New Directions Publishing Corporation
80 Eighth Avenue, New York 10011

ndbooks.com

I thought you were an anchor in the drift of the world;
but no: there isn't an anchor anywhere.
There isn't an anchor in the drift of the world. Oh no.
I thought you were. Oh no. The drift of the world.

—William Bronk

CONTENTS

BE WITH

The political begins in intimacy

SON

It's not the mirror that is draped, but
what remains unspoken between us. Why

say anything about death, inevitability, how
the body comes to deploy the myriad worm

as if it were a manageable concept not
searing exquisite singularity. To serve it up like

a eulogy or a tale of my or your own
suffering. Some kind of self-abasement.

And so we continue waking to a decapitated sun and trees
continue to irk me. The heart of charity

bears its own set of genomes. You lug a bacterial swarm
in the crook of your knee, and through my guts

writhe helminth parasites. Who was ever only themselves?
At Leptis Magna, when your mother & I were young, we came across

statues of gods with their faces and feet cracked off by vandals. But
for the row of guardian Medusa heads. No one so brave to deface those.

When she spoke, when your mother spoke, even the leashed
greyhound stood transfixed. I stood transfixed.

I gave my life to strangers; I kept it from the ones I love.
Her one arterial child. It is just in you her blood runs.

BECKONED

At which point my grief-sounds ricocheted outside of language.

Something like a drifting swarm of bees.

At which point in the tetric silence that followed

I was swarmed by those bees and lost consciousness.

At which point there was no way out for me either.

At which point I carried on in a semi-coma, dreaming I was awake,

avoiding friends and puking, plucking stingers from my face and arms.

At which point her voice was pinned to a backdrop of vaporous color.

At which point the crane's bustles flared.

At which point, coming to, I knew I'd pay the whole flag-pull fare.

At which point the driver turned and said it doesn't need to be

your fault for it to break you.

At which point without any lurching commencement,

he began to play a vulture-bone flute.

At which point I grew old and it was like ripping open the beehive
    with my hands again.

At which point I conceived a realm more real than life.

At which point there was at least some possibility.

Some possibility, in which I didn't believe, of being with her once more.

To write *You*
existed me
would not be merely
a deaf translation.

For there is no
sequel to the passage when
I saw—*as you would*
never again
be revealed—you see me
as I would never
again be revealed.

Where I stand now
before the throne of
glory, the script
must remain hidden. Where,
but in the utterance itself?

Born halt and
blind, hooped-in by
obligations, aware
of the stare of
the animal inside, I
hide behind mixed
instrumentalities
as behind a square
of crocodile scute—

while cyanide drifts
from clouds to
the rivers. And in this
too might be seen
a figuration
of the human,
another intimately
lethal gesture of our
common existence.

Though I also wear
my life into death, the
ugliness I originate
outlives me.

DEADOUT

I.

Gets out his dab rig and shatter
At once at its mercy and in control of it

The bull snake lifted the terrarium cover
About three feet six from snout to vent

Youngbloods metaphorizing death
What kind of clue do they have

Her scent: vinegar, zinc oxide, and hinoki cypress
He dreamed of it awake dreams of it

Watching another season of Spanky Wankers
Only made his fillings ache

So now he's got reptile dysfunction
Me too, says the dust.

Motorcycle parked in the handicapped spot
He regards the forest of standing dead snags

II.

Youngbloods metaphorizing death
Only made his fillings ache

The bull snake lifted the terrarium cover
He dreamed of it awake dreams of it

Gets out his dab rig and shatter
Me too, says the dust

About three feet six from snout to vent
So now he's got reptile dysfunction

Her scent: vinegar, zinc oxide, and hinoki cypress
At once at its mercy and in control of it

What kind of clue do they have
He regards the forest of standing dead snags

Watching another season of Spanky Wankers
Motorcycle parked in the handicapped spot

CARBONIZED FOREST

The eye that was open on Friday.

The portent and the portent's flensed hide. Ribbons of flesh

swarming downward. Like a school of leeches

deserting some unlit cataclysm.

And a briary phantom there, Stygian, erect.

Saying, here is the untranslation of the world.

Mounted on a spire of form.

The disembarkation of abyss. Fragmentary sputtering.

And what you thought were dark whiptails of illumination

were bristles from a shaved bear

being milked for bile in a rusting cage. Nested

among the mesh of soft translucent sounds

fallen from your lips, the

vestiges of someone's breathing.

ENTENDERMENT

You could see: her   consciousness was in her skin
While his primary material   was weightlessness
She candled   eggs for Petaluma Poultry
And daydreamed   of stars glowering
In the Prawn Nebula's ultraviolet light
He saw himself   a victim of place
Among shirtless gods   playing frisbee on the green
Oh death, he mumbled (in his sleep), I'm   coming for you
It's true, la vida   es caprichosa y puñetera
Full of unresolved sevenths   and ninths
So like Su   Hui's infinite poem

And once when sipping   water he coughed,
She started to   laugh, mistaking his gesture
Every event drags   loss behind it

                    Dark, be bright
                    There's nightshade in my brain

They meant to shut their door   to the setting sun
But her knees   poked through the soap bubbles
While he stayed out late   lying on his back
Under the ultraviolet light of the Prawn Nebula

Behind   a drawn curtain
The nurse   cursed
Giving voice   to his own inarticulacy
Trauma   brings its singular sharpness.
Everyone sees her   in his eyes

He offers a cigarette   for the dog to eat
And goes back   to metronoming

Re-coupled   to the common lag of friends
Tic Tacs   rattle in his pocket
He's breathing tequila   fumes at 9 a.m.
Unreadable but not   ambiguous
Like hounds   yowling at the horizon
Below the Prawn Nebula's ultraviolet light

She wrote, *Life*   *feels life in language*
Her mind's voluptuousness   so substantial
Adjectives   fizz away
He observes   the shadow thrown
By nothing is thrown   by the nothing he is

MADONNA DEL PARTO

And then smelling it,
feeling it before
the sound even reaches
him, he kneels at
cliff's edge and for the
first time, turns his
head toward the now
visible falls that
gush over a quarter
mile of uplifted sheet-
granite across the valley
and he pauses,
lowering his eyes
for a moment, unable
to withstand the
tranquility—vast, unencumbered,
terrifying, and primal. That
naked river
enthroned upon
the massif altar,
bowed cypresses
congregating on both
sides of sun-gleaming rock, a rip
in the fabric of the ongoing
forest from which rises—
as he tries to stand, tottering, half-
paralyzed—a shifting
rainbow volatilized by
ceaseless explosion.

ON A SENTENCE BY FERNANDA MELCHOR

¿Qué es lo más cabrón que te ha pasado en la vida?
The most fucked-up thing to happen to me?
Addled by busyness, I crumpled my life and let it drop
and then I outlived my life, rocking
on my misery like a cypress in the wind. I watched
stars emerge from a black egg. Lucidity
of loss. Someone came to tell me the spider
vibrating on its long legs in the ceiling corner
over my desk doesn't exist now. It is wedged
between the violent uninterruptedness
of one single day and the void I discovered
inside myself. Forehead tautening with self-pity.
I said, You think you know me, but you don't
know me from Adam's goat. And she said,
I do, and you are one and the same thing.

STEPPING OUT OF THE LIGHT

Bleaching the
spaces between
each trunk, fog de-
lineates, from
a vast of green,
the silhouette of
each pine
on the slope.

Maybe it's like that,
only all along it was
obscured by what?
Rush, distraction? Fog.
A pine. Querying
grosbeak. Something
shifts. You find
yourself in another
world you weren't
looking for where
what you see is that
you have always been
the wolves
at the door. Left

ajar, gaping, your own
door. And you burst
in as the Mangler,
you gouge out
your right eye which
hath offended. And you

burst in as the Great
Liar gorging
on your own flesh
and as Won't
Let Go who shreds
your tendons, gnaws
your femur. You can't
stop bursting in,
coming upon yourself
alone, vulnerable, in the
privacy of your dying,
bending to pick up
with a tissue a crushed spider

from the bedroom floor,
half-sensing in your solar
plexus the forces
of that which cannot yet
be sussed, discovering yourself
once again already
to have been inside something
like an equation with
a remainder, a deodand, a
reminder of the impossibility
of reconcilement—
to what? Once again. Forgive
yourself, they say, but
after you forgive
what you have lived,
what is left? You can't

set aside the jigger
of the present from
the steady pour of hours
or even differentiate
trails of ants
scurrying through some
massive subterranean network
from the shredded
remains of a galaxy
backlit by star glow. Time

to close the door you think
but your face is changed,
so many crow's feet. You
must be on
to the next stage
in which you begin
to recognize
your mortal body,
that nexus of your various
holds on the world, as
repository of every-
thing you didn't know
you took in, human
and not, all of it
charged and reactant
which accounts for the trembling
in your hands as now
you discern the
body of your body—

like a still,
hanging bell
that catches and concentrates
each ghostly, ambient
reverberation.

WHAT IT SOUNDS LIKE

As grains sort inside a schist

An ancient woodland indicator called *dark dog's mercury*

River like liquid shale

And white-tipped black lizard-turds on the blue wall

For a loss that every other loss fits inside

Picking at a mole until it bleeds

As the day heaves forward on faked determinations

If it's not all juxtaposition, she asked, what is the binding agent?

Creepy always to want to pin words on "the emotional experience"

Azure hoplia cockchafer, the caddis worm, the bee-louse, blister
beetle, assassin bug

The recriminations swarm around sunset

When it was otherwise quiet all the way around

You who were given a life, what did you make of it?

WHERE ONCE A SOLID HOUSE

The voice singing in the kitchen   isn't your voice
There is   no voice singing in the kitchen

Opens last night's   pizza box
Its dry   strings of cheese splayed
Like tendons   in a crushed hand

From your deep I've spilled   into shallows
Flopping   asphyxiated
My speech   a paroxysm

How I wish   you are here
As I try   to gather the periphery
The places that impressed   themselves on us and
It all returns   strangely as fog
Rising just to flatten   under the bridges

When you asked for less   rigor more entenderment
When you asked   for more—

Knowing: not as recitation   but as
The unhinging   somatic event
Though now all   my memories begin with outcomes
As in Ferdowsi's   *Shahnameh*
Our annals blend into landscapes   where they took place
The protagonists so loose   their molecules mix
With swaths   of water with earth and light

For *surely the people*   *is grass* like they say
Even here   at Punto de las Culebras
No bitterness   no envy no greed

Unless   this is something else altogether
Akin to turning leaves   with a stumpripper only
To find a   striking pit viper

THE SOUNDING

What closes and then
luminous? What opens
and then dark? And into
what do you stumble
but this violet
extinction? With
froth on your lips.
8:16 a.m. The morning's
sleepy face

rolls its million
eyes. Migrating flocks
of your likesame species
incandesce
into transparency.
A birdwatcher lifts

her binoculars. The con-
tinuous with or without
your words
situates you here
(here (here)) even while
you knuckle your eyes
in disbelief. Those

voices you love (human
and not), can you
hear their echoes
hissing away like
fiery scale
from an ingot hammered
on some
blacksmith's anvil?
And behind those
voices, *what is that*
blowing
the valves of your ears open
as black rain,
not in torrents, but
ceaselessly comes
unchecked out of everywhere
with nothing
to slacken it.

FIRST BALLAD: A WREATH

after St. John of the Cross

In the beginning the Word   was as being
In happiness   infinitely the Word possessed

The same Word being was   said to be beginning
Beginninglessly   it went on

A sum caroming   through fervid void
For the Word   from the outset

Always was   conceiving
Concentrating its   consequence for

Glory in the Word   possessed the being
And all of being's substance it   gleaned from the Word

Lover in beloved in   the other one went on
And that love which entwined them was of the same

Sum two   voices one beloved
Among two   and in them each

One happiness   rendered them one lover
A splendor un-   confessed—gleaming

As two possess one being   each alone possessed it
Each of them in love   a plenum of the Word

Whose being each   twined around the other
Beyond comprehension   an ineffable knot

Such fervid love   entwined the two together
In one voice both possessed   a plenum of the world
The more that love was one   the more of love there was

ARCHAIC MANO

In (microscopic) pocks of a
  palmsize basalt stone
    traces of green corn purslane
     (snakefat) and piñon fuse
      with smeared roots
       and beeweed pollen
        (ochredust) which drifts
      summerlong into the
     scalp of a woman kneeling
    (intent) and bent over a
   lightbitten stone basin
  her muscles flexed
 trapezius to
triceps the wrist   *(thin like yours)*
working a short
 orbital swipe hand-
  stone taking
   the curve
    of palm (cupped)
     and her torso's weight
      fallingthrough while
     swallows dive and
      veer along the sheer
       cliff the warm
        scabbed heel of her
        palm bears down
        (heel of palm) onto
         and into the skirlingsound
        stone merged
       with the hand

                    that grinds it
                    wheel-wise,
                    the maker (breath-
                    blown) alive
                        in her tool (lithe)
                        flies fuss and
                        land her hair
                    falling across her
(as your hair)   eyes radiant-   (across your eyes)
                    upbeat leaftrilled and
                into this cadence
                is inset
                the slower cadence
                to which
            she rocks her baby
        when he cries
    and all the variable
        tempos of her breath,   (breathe)
            her body's measure
            countless (breaths)
                decibels of fullness
                daysutterance and
                stress all this
                    pressed (against basalt),
                    vesicles into the stone

                    into the (pocked) stone

                                                        35

goes a rabbit hair
brushed from the hand
that scraped
the hide in late
eyelong afternoon when
red ants pour from
holes in rocky soil
ticking across fluff grass
(square-headed ants) toward
a garden where three
turkeys peck those (leaf-
eating) ants (so that
the garden greensup)
a minor victory
that registers
in the eyes   *(and behind her eyes)*
of the woman   *(your eyes)*
who scuffs
stone on stone
in the floodbuckling
blare of violence
and time
that pockets her light
in my (our) light
as my pupil narrows
in its lens and I bend   *(lord, I kneel)*

(before your stone)

in a clearing
to pick up
and weigh this density
hawkglide wingspread
my hand holding what
millennia ago
her hand held
who winks out as
I come clear (to
whom?) on a
green hillside
where someone kneels
in the now (even
now) beyond
our (stillflow) looking

TELL THEM NO

"The essence of the thing is often
in the flash." —Clarice Lispector

Like some
freshly emergent
thing, he clung
to her
until the chitin
of his
limbs hardened
and fluid
flowing
from his eyes
and through the
struts of his
wings crystallized.

What a good
human life
looks like. In
bed as
out. An extreme
conjunction.

When I first wet
and swirled in its
cream the sheeny
badger-hair
shaving brush you
gave me as a gift, its
shocking feral musk
locked on to my face.

Fog all morning, impressive
gray hat-band under
mottled crown of mountain,
its top edge sliding
south and thin
steam from the Petaluma
dairy spewing in
the same direction.

Not to
choose one
happiness over
another but to
keep choosing
an Appomattox
unhappiness?

Stumbling again
dumbly
home into the
line of my
own questioning.

Carried too far
off course? As
when the caterpillar
carrying wasp
maggots turns
to wasp maggots
currying
the caterpillar's
corpse.

So hard—no
matter how bad
expressed—
your own or
other's pain,
undressed—to
            turn from.

The cabinet
door's squeaky
dactylic remark:
Hap-pi-ness?
But each morning
the same
scene. A lizard
doing push-ups
on the same
baked rock.
My unsalvable
inclination for
daily routine.

Not far
from the right
metaphor:
a cigar coming
apart in the train
station toilet.

A lo que una buena
vida humana
se asemeja. Una
conjunción extrema.

She said suffering wasn't necessary.
He said it was the gateway.
She said, Drag it back where it came from.
She said, You call everybody baby.
He said, It's like free money, sort of.
She said he said to just stand here.

It means just
what it feels like
it means.

Their dog's deep gaze,
her stomach gurgling.
Clitoris plumping under pressure.
Was that a pump knot on his forehead?
Long doctor-office afternoons
drained her life. Hummingbird?
His suede jacket went dark at the collar
with oil from her hair.

Then scratched my
arm with my teeth,
nicking the cap
of the eggshell and
taking the larvae
of recognition into
my mouth.

To parcel it
out, the self
as introduction.
Who am I *is*
what I can do.

At some point, change
results in a retrogression
the mind sees
as failure. A disgusting
odor cultivated. So
I search for your
face with a file-like
roughness as though
for a resonant edge.

At his solar
plexus, the
elevator
cable snaps.
It's when I lie
down at night,
she says,
my heart
races.

The flowers I
pick too
late hiss
in the vase,
missing you.

When what is
demanded is
change so
fundamental
only another
personality could
accomplish it.

What blind gnawing
mandibled head
was chewing up the silken
thread we thought
would guide us
back to bed?

Are you
hyperventilating?
she calls
from the next
room.

Pasted-on
conversational
replies.

It lopes and turns,
lopes and turns, lopes
and turns to look
back toward the
road where
she stands
immobilized, as
though watching.

Is there nightshade
in my brain? That
I conceive
your consequence
as some stage in
my need?

Dear spider, in
this house eight
legs are too many.

A few days later
their bliss grew
an impenetrable
skin. Then dissolved
itself completely,
the liquid content of
that skin turning
to a sort of jelly
from which erupts
a new creature
whose organs
lack any identity
with what came
before.

Have I lived
something stupid?
Am I the coward
responsible for
nothing?

Suspended
between north
and south,
claims to ex-
perience pain,
and so
sustains
an orchestral
tension.

Saturation point.
When your own misery preens
you against the misery
of others.

Keeps his hat on as
he enters, but thoughtfully
wipes his feet. The women
at the far table are carpenters
wearing kneepads. On the
room's near side,
a rough caste of men
sit conspiratorially close
and track each other
from the corners
of their eyes. Contagious
guffaws punctuating
brief jokes.

At the bar, honey
bottle in a bowl of
water. *Account
of the ants.* Sign
says Hangovers
Installed & Serviced.

Standing in a wind of
diesel fuel waiting
for his luggage. Shaking
silently, mouth agape.
Pulping his eyes
with his knuckles.

The spectacularization
of the trivial, bad
faith hilarity, the
imitation of the imitation's
imitation intensifying
the suck of a vacuum.

I hear the busyness in
their voices, they hear
the busyness in my voice.
To be oblivious, in some
manifold danger. And
so one lives.

Like how
early around?
she asked.

Here is a steel wire with a ring at one end.
Intuition of the infinite.
At its other end I've screwed a conical cap
with sharp cutting edges at the base.
The infinite always intuited against
the background of the infinite. If
it doesn't serve to open up
a sound, the particular sound for
instance of my lips releasing
your name, then a gland may be involved
and another kind of treatment
called for. Won't you please
toss a handful of your infinite
phosphene into my gloom-sopped eyes.

A copper-iridescent laughter finishes up your sentence.

This last, contemporary stage,
my stage, the stage that anticipates,
that counter-actualizes my
contingency here, my under-
regarded privilege, this stage
will reach its maturity today
causing a slight rise
in temperature followed by
inflammation around the throat
and jaw where numerous red
nodules swell with serous
fluid. Doc's advice: *Don't probe
them with your fingertips. Even the
greatest care proves insufficient.*

Didn't lose
his own but
found another
voice that
didn't fit.

"If you want
to throw in
some dirt," the priest
addressed the widower
and his child generally
but did not
complete
the sentence.

Carrying
the rat of
affliction between
my teeth for
all to see. Just.
Try. To. Take. It.
From. Me.

His readiest emotion
was righteousness. Self-
absorbed error. But
now it's terror.

Siphon the real
into the practical: that's
what the drugs do.

Field flecked purple with nightshade
and lupine. Ruby-throated bird
at the bottlebrush bloom. One's
own mediocrity sharpens it.

Dog baying in tune
with the siren. Maybe the
couple will arrive yet
in time for events
to assign them
another meaning. As
she disengages the hooks
from the eyelets, he stiffens.

EVAPORACIÓN: A BORDER HISTORY

Paisanos they call
      roadrunners, brothers of the land. A dozen
Mexican corpses marooned
         under desert sun.
    In cottonwoods by the river,
zone-tailed hawks squeal. Visible
      desde el aire, the craquelure of
an abandoned runway
           overlies
         toxic waste and unexploded munitions.
    Bordered by purple and yellow
bloomstalks: lechuguilla.
         Volcanic chimneys up-thrust
            from barren flats. Agleam
     in a basalt outcrop, fist-size
        feldspar crystals. The old raiding trails
     from Comanchería convergen
en un path packed by hoofprints.

Alarming *ki-dear ki-dear* of a
Cassin's kingbird on the
barbed fence. 150 miles
surveilled by a white aerostat
que se parece a una ballena. Between those peaks
sits Panther Laccolith. Both vaqueros
staked out naked, screaming on an ant hill.
Female katydid waving her foreleg tympanum
at the stridulating males. The fine-
grained intrusion that veined the mountain
also silled Paint Gap Hill.
Su caballo tembla en agonía, pinned to the ground by a spear.
Hovering over the field, a flock of crested flycatchers.
The border-patrol dog lifts its leg
at the tire of the Skywagon. Cercas de coachwhip
van paralelas al camino. Chihuahua
Trail following Alameda Creek. They call it
horse-crippler cactus.

Vietnam-era seismic probes
enterrados bajo estas propiedades privadas. Lava-rock
rims the sides.
Give it a break, mockingbird.
El Despoblado. Giant yucca and bunch grass.
And what ventures into the afternoon heat? Only Pharoah ants.
Only the insulated darkling beetle.
En los dos lados del pavimiento, magnetic sensors
registran movimiento y dirección. Evening
cicadas eclipse tree crickets.
A thousand head of cattle
driven below the trachyte hoodoos. It nibbles
a prickly pear: cottontail at dusk.
Human contraband at dusk. Famous
for their dwarf fauna, estos estratos fósiles. Depositions of
carnage, catches
of light. Our legacy
mission. A carcass of
the unspoken
aullando.

RUTH

Her husband lifeless
in chair facing
TV, whole days
mute, her own mind,
her hearing,
shot. *And it won't
get any better. Absolutely
nothing to look
forward to*, she says
to whom if
not you?

Wearing two identical
left shoes. *No one
believes I don't
dye my hair*, she remarks
for the umpteenth
time. Point taken, I'm
grayer than my
mother though
in the mirror I see
her face, her small
dark eyes.

Five states north, he
wonders what
causes the
swishing
he hears behind
his mother's
voice: she's
down on the
floor, the phone
in one hand
and with
the other,
she must be
scratching the
tumorous dog
whose paw
convulsively
rakes the carpet.

green case on the nightstand
glasses on a Redskins lanyard

green glasses case
containing one hearing aid

minus its battery on the nightstand
glasses on a Redskins lanyard

in the green grass
under one of many bird feeders

in the backyard thronging
with blurred mute birds

Occasional muculent chortling
or choking and steady
beep of the EKG.

The beak-hard
determination to
be a good person,
what happened
to that? How
is it true
I have to
go now? She's lost
my name, but the
occasion of my
presence begs
more. Who is my
mother now I am
unspoken for?

So take her hand, walking in
the garden: an animal moment of warmth
she won't recall after our sit. Voracious
starlings ride a swinging cage of suet.
That signal enthusiasm in her eyes
muddles with torment. Choose whatever
you will and the disease
still wins. Like a heavy shawl,
the shadow of cloud drags across
mountains on the horizon. Maybe I've
misread her expression.

To plunge into love as into a sidewalk.
Came awake as though I were a siren going off.
The ghastliness of putting food in my
mouth, my belly gurgling
like so many horse-leeches. And so
days-to-come will crack open without you,
dropping their yolk over places you walked.
And the white lowly primrose will foam
wild like some scrap of your happiness
refusing to abandon me. Blah blah. The
mirror in the shrine is memory. All
you lived adjusts now and is lived back
in me here on earth. A flock of geese
sifts through the barrow pit. Post-puke
acid sears my throat.

To find the present breaking itself
loose from the sequence of events, bolting
through gaps in the corral of context and
carrying its befuddled rider

                    into an expanding plain of brumous outlines.

* * *

How she fights the sleeping pill, to stay up with me as I drive back
from the beach, to keep talking, to speak and be spoken to: the
assurance of voices, even her own now druggy iterative slur which is
like low birdsong, a blind inquiry in twilight—*is someone there?*—and a
claim she is alive, here in the seat beside me, her seatbelt around her
as she overcomes the pill, the devious obstacle course, the drowsiness
I administered in order to drive her four hours home this evening,
to concentrate on driving, to save my pollen-swollen and mucus-
inflamed throat from the overtime shift of talk, to stay the repetitive
questions, her struggle among scraps and familiar names torn
from faces and feelings, the cipher-names of her husband and her
grandchildren, a language of blanks, I drive with my left hand on the
wheel, the other massaging the loose skin of *her* hands, feeling for
the tightened cords in her palms, bands of fascia that curl her fingers
forward, and when I think she's finally fallen asleep, her face up-tilted
and drawn, as we cross Indian River Inlet where she'd often, with
my father, fished for flounder from the Grady-White whose single
outboard, pumped and primed, they'd startled into coughs of blue
smoke in the canal back in Bethany hours earlier and piloted through
the gauntlet of buoys—*red right return*—that drew it through Assa-
woman Bay, past Harpoon Hanna's, and into the yawning Atlantic—
when I start to pull my hand away, she tightens her grip, not opening
her eyes, maybe in reflex, holding on to her will to be awake with
me, her son, whom she knows, whom she thanks now in her almost
sleep, her narcotic fatigue, in the spreading murk of the pill I coaxed
her to swallow so that the trip might be easier while she rides beside
me, holding on.

* * *

Sitting on the edge of the bed with her shirt and pants off, she reaches behind to unclasp her bra. I help her stand and draw her underwear down, and she lists to one side in pain, though she doesn't complain.

This is how she wants to go to the bathroom, naked, before we put her pajamas on. Never either shy or proud of her body. Even in my childhood, I understood she regarded the body as implement. Whatever the psychological traumas my sisters and I metabolized, we grew up at ease in our bodies, unembarrassed by nakedness.

Before me, my mother looks plumper than she does in clothes, but staggering toward the bathroom, reaching for the doorknob, she is a splotched drama of mortality, her buttocks collapsed into folds, the scar from her vertebroplasty lost in a constellation of liver spots, her waist overcome by sagging flesh.

A memory: in La Paz, I saw the old Aymara wave backwards over their shoulders when they spoke of the future. And to reference the past, make sweeping forward motions with their hands. The Aymara word for eye, front, and sight signals *past*, while the word for *future* means back or behind. In my mother's body, too, her front is the past and her back, the future.

She sits and I bunch pajama-bottoms over her feet, one at a time, and pull them up as she bends forward to stand in elaborate slow motion. Another world's wounded crane.

* * *

To listen to each repetition with renewed attentiveness as if it were
the first occasion, to forget you've heard it before and to receive her
words as her first words or her last ones, for she repeats things not
only because she's forgotten but also so they will be remembered.
To come into a rhythm of farewell with her, marking it, relishing its
periodicity, in order to crack open another kind of love inside the old,
familiar love, a vast of acceptance, without condition, akin to what a
mother might feel for her child.

***

Want to but can't. I can't die, she says, and her eyebrows
furrow, expatiating the point. A chiming
of patient monitors like electronic crickets
in perpetual night. Or a subaltern intelligence. Code
red is clear. Did Karin put lipstick on you this morning?
A quarter turn of the petcock on the O_2 tank. We brought
dinner from The Quotidian Pain. Outside
the hospital window, stars glowing in the ultraviolet
light of the Prawn Nebula. *It's you who are.* What?
A hummingbird, she says. My lord, in heart, and let
the health go round. Though I am so far already
in your gifts.

LITTORAL ZONE

Entrance

Whether the blackness is interior—pelagic & vegetal there, organic &
intestinal there—or mere background for such shapeliness of globes:
spangled with lampyrid glow, airy with striate foliation, and nowhere
stricked-off level.

The shapes are white as tissue? Gauze?
No, they are transparent and white.
They are membranous?
They are milky.
And the vertical thrust of their entanglement?
Shows they coalesced under the influence.

Suspiration from our
lung-thicket. Lengths of
limbs in limbo on
the furrowed sheets:
so love buds again, a-
gain in trembles above
this earth-smoke.

Exit

A swarm of projectile bobbles lifts (effervescent) over the lip into a
grim rictus and drifts there, lost along the spackled backwall.

*Such light, like ivory spokeshaves flared. And knobby florets caroming
radially over the curve, the curve extremetizing distance, distance weighing
against foreground. Were such improvisation to rise spontaneously out of
itself, with whom might it be shared?*

Fuegos fatuos: we cast
double shadows in Pantone
blacks. My salamandrine
longing stutter-caught
on your nocturnal gorges.
Until you're sub-
tracted from the visible
escarpment and I'm a throbbing
waste-heap of ghost.

Entrance

They cruise white mesas moored in night, bumping opalescent
dripstone. Cave onyx. No apparent source of light.

Struck by the pointlessness of comparison, but what more can one want?
For seeing not to degenerate into habit? And what if the demands for
another kind of seeing cannot be regarded as what we take to be "seeing?" As
one turns away, the retained image vitiates what swings into view.

My levorotatory isomers
going optically active, erotic. Sweeping
across pelagic intimations, your
apprising glance: entwined
stalks, we swale against the wall.
My fingers nest in your hollow:
a flotsam of hieroglyphics
in tadpole murk.

Exit

Boles, water circles, barnacle scars, the radiant circles clash, wrinkling a skin, a skin over what? The involute dimension surges from labradorite sheen, a wave-shadow scarred with cracks, and the lit edge sputtering vapor.

If a mountain lion could speak, who wouldn't understand her? On the path, yellow jackets and Painted Ladies alight where a seep darkens loam. A gleam on the slickensides. Sanctified stone.

The siren's sound
surrounds us at
the siltation
zone while
lightning delineates
pleats of night. Then
the sting: I'm
paralyzed, you've
disappeared. Only
my eyes. Eyes. Widening.

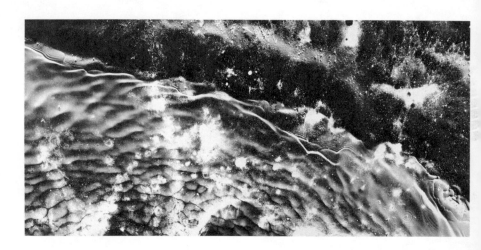

Entrance

Glacéed by fervor of sun, a carbonized melt. Granular at the liquid
edge. A shoreline cuffed with foam along dark cordilleras.

And what experience corroborates this image? Is it measured in centimeters
or miles? Or does the expression of measurement depend upon some metaphor?
Assuming there exists a place that corresponds at all. But what if there never
were such "place" and it was always modes of exchange, like months later
paying for a funeral?

The reach of neural
conduct nears
threshold momentums
in your breath, our
pooled smolder. Un-
sodden bloom: inversion
puddle. Just our wet
flesh saves us
from the scorch
of annunciation.

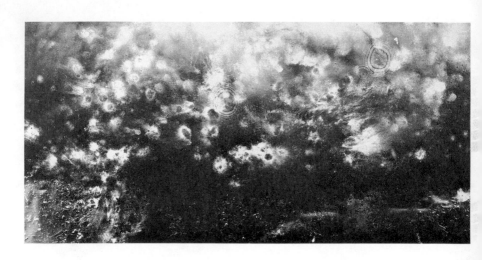

Exit

Mobbed phosphorescence, gaseous swarm. And breathbeats blazed into an invisible integument. To begin in intimacy on this volcanic tuff. Here to cling.

For though we have no criterion for how to see and are not sure what we are seeing, we are plunged into sensation. As into a novel ache. But what ever has dispassionate description delivered?

Your impact marks
throng the resin
of my mind. Declension,
a focal spasm. When your
eyelids release their tension,
nocturnal pods, in-
vertebrate and
membranous, surge
into my dreams. From
afar, do you see me now
briefly here in this phantasmic
standoff riding
pain's whirlforms?

ACKNOWLEDGMENTS

"Son" was published in *The New Yorker*, edited by Kevin Young.

"Beckoned" was published in *Harper's*, edited by Ben Lerner.

"Carbonized Forest" is for the artist Richard Fishman.

"Madonna del Parto" was published in *Poem-a-Day*, Academy of American Poets, edited by Meghan O'Rourke & Evie Shockley.

"On a Sentence by Fernanda Melchor" was published in *The Nation*, edited by Carmen Giménez Smith & Stephanie Burt.

"Stepping Out of the Light" and "What It Sounds Like" were published in *Poetry*, edited by Don Share.

"The Sounding" was published in *Resistance, Rebellion, Life: 50 Poems Now*, edited by Amit Majmudar, Knopf, 2017.

An earlier form of "First Ballad: a Wreath" was published in *Mānoa*, edited by Frank Stewart.

The late poet Jake Adam York sent me from Colorado a *mano*, a handstone used by ancient Pueblo for grinding meal, etc. He asked me to write a poem for it. At the inspired instigation of Steve Alpert (thank you, Steve), an earlier form of "Archaic Mano" was included in a collaboration with glass artist Michael Rogers, ceramicist Rick Hirsch, and poet C.D. Wright. Poems and sculptural works were exhibited at the University Gallery, Rochester Institute of Technology in 2012 and at the Cohen Gallery, Granoff Center, Brown University, 2013. The earlier version of the poem was published in *Lana Turner: a Journal of Poetry and Opinion*, edited by Calvin Bedient.

Some of the poems in "Tell Them No" were published in a collaboration with Gus Van Sant called "Thirteen Flowers," *NeueJournal*, edited by Dominic Teja Sidhu. Others in this series were published in *Sijo: an International Journal of Poetry and Song*, edited by David McCann, Wayne de Fremery & Dan Disney.

"Evaporación: a Border History" was first published in *Hwaet!*, edited by Neil Astley, Bloodaxe Books (UK), 2016; republished in *Atlantic Drift*, edited by James Byrne & Robert Sheppard, Arc Publications, 2017, and in *Poetry International*, edited by Ilya Kaminsky.

The poems in "Ruth" were first published in *Conjunctions*,
edited by Bradford Morrow.

Six poems from "Littoral Zone," with photographs by Michael Flomen,
were published in earlier drafts in *Alligatorzine*, edited by Kurt Devrese.

As after certain events, everything changes, many of the poems cited above
are different now than at the time of their publication in magazines.

Thanks for the care of your words Calvin Bedient, James Byrne, Lynn Keller,
Pilar Fraile Amador & Esther Ramón. In gratefulness for your friendship: Brenda Hillman,
Bob Hass, Dan Beachy-Quick, Arthur Sze, Sharon Olds, Laura Mullen, Valerie Mejer,
Mike Perrow, Lida Junghans, Brady Earnhart, Anna Deeny, Don Mee Choi, Brian Evenson,
Pura López Colomé, Cole Swensen, Edmundo Garrido, Carmen Giménez Smith,
Christina Davis, Declan Spring, and Eliot Weinberger.

Thanks to the Community of Writers at Squaw Valley
where some of these poems gushed forth.

New Directions Paperbooks—a partial listing

César Aira, Ema, the Captive
  An Episode in the Life of a Landscape Painter
  Ghosts
Will Alexander, The Sri Lankan Loxodrome
Osama Alomar, The Teeth of the Comb
Guillaume Apollinaire, Selected Writings
Paul Auster, The Red Notebook
Honoré de Balzac, Colonel Chabert
Djuna Barnes, Nightwood
Jorge Barón Biza, The Desert and Its Seed
Charles Baudelaire, The Flowers of Evil*
Bei Dao, City Gate, Open Up
Nina Berberova, The Ladies From St. Petersburg
Mei-Mei Berssenbrugge, Hello, the Roses
Max Blecher, Adventures in Immediate Irreality
Roberto Bolaño, By Night in Chile
  Distant Star
  Nazi Literature in the Americas
Jorge Luis Borges, Labyrinths
  Seven Nights
Coral Bracho, Firefly Under the Tongue*
Kamau Brathwaite, Ancestors
Basil Bunting, Complete Poems
Anne Carson, Antigonick
  Glass, Irony & God
Horacio Castellanos Moya, Senselessness
Camilo José Cela, Mazurka for Two Dead Men
Louis-Ferdinand Céline
  Death on the Installment Plan
  Journey to the End of the Night
Rafael Chirbes, On the Edge
Inger Christensen, alphabet
Jean Cocteau, The Holy Terrors
Julio Cortázar, Cronopios & Famas
  62: A Model Kit
Robert Creeley, If I Were Writing This
Guy Davenport, 7 Greeks
Osamu Dazai, No Longer Human
H.D., Selected Poems
  Tribute to Freud
Helen DeWitt, The Last Samurai
Daša Drndić, Belladonna
Robert Duncan, Selected Poems
Eça de Queirós, The Illustrious House of Ramires
William Empson, 7 Types of Ambiguity
Matthias Énard, Compass
Shusaku Endo, Deep River

Jenny Erpenbeck, The End of Days
  Go, Went, Gone
  Visitation
Lawrence Ferlinghetti
  A Coney Island of the Mind
F. Scott Fitzgerald, The Crack-Up
  On Booze
Forrest Gander, The Trace
Romain Gary, Promise at Dawn
Henry Green, Concluding
John Hawkes, Travesty
Felisberto Hernández, Piano Stories
Hermann Hesse, Siddhartha
Takashi Hiraide, The Guest Cat
Yoel Hoffman, Moods
Susan Howe, My Emily Dickinson
  Debths
Bohumil Hrabal, I Served the King of England
Qurratulain Hyder, River of Fire
Sonallah Ibrahim, That Smell
Rachel Ingalls, Mrs. Caliban
Christopher Isherwood, The Berlin Stories
Fleur Jaeggy, I Am the Brother of XX
Alfred Jarry, Ubu Roi
B.S. Johnson, House Mother Normal
James Joyce, Stephen Hero
Franz Kafka, Amerika: The Man Who Disappeared
  Investigations of a Dog
Yasunari Kawabata, Dandelions
John Keene, Counternarratives
Alexander Kluge, Temple of the Scapegoat
Laszlo Krasznahorkai, Satantango
  Seiobo There Below
  War and War
Ryszard Krynicki, Magnetic Point
Eka Kurniawan, Beauty Is a Wound
Mme. de Lafayette, The Princess of Clèves
Lautréamont, Maldoror
Denise Levertov, Selected Poems
Li Po, Selected Poems
Clarice Lispector, The Hour of the Star
  Near to the Wild Heart
  The Passion According to G. H.
Federico García Lorca, Selected Poems*
  Three Tragedies
Nathaniel Mackey, Splay Anthem
Xavier de Maistre, Voyage Around My Room
Stéphane Mallarmé, Selected Poetry and Prose*

Javier Marías, Your Face Tomorrow (3 volumes)
Harry Mathews, The Solitary Twin
Bernadette Mayer, Works & Days
Carson McCullers, The Member of the Wedding
Thomas Merton, New Seeds of Contemplation
  The Way of Chuang Tzu
Henri Michaux, A Barbarian in Asia
Dunya Mikhail, The Beekeeper
Henry Miller, The Colossus of Maroussi
  Big Sur & The Oranges of Hieronymus Bosch
Yukio Mishima, Confessions of a Mask
  Death in Midsummer
Eugenio Montale, Selected Poems*
Vladimir Nabokov, Laughter in the Dark
  Nikolai Gogol
  The Real Life of Sebastian Knight
Raduan Nassar, A Cup of Rage
Pablo Neruda, The Captain's Verses*
  Love Poems*
  Residence on
Charles Olson, Selected Writings
George Oppen, New Collected Poems
Wilfred Owen, Collected Poems
Michael Palmer, The Laughter of the Sphinx
Nicanor Parra, Antipoems*
Boris Pasternak, Safe Conduct
Kenneth Patchen
  Memoirs of a Shy Pornographer
Octavio Paz, Poems of Octavio Paz
Victor Pelevin, Omon Ra
Alejandra Pizarnik
  Extracting the Stone of Madness
Ezra Pound, The Cantos
  New Selected Poems and Translations
Raymond Queneau, Exercises in Style
Qian Zhongshu, Fortress Besieged
Raja Rao, Kanthapura
Herbert Read, The Green Child
Kenneth Rexroth, Selected Poems
Keith Ridgway, Hawthorn & Child
Rainer Maria Rilke
  Poems from the Book of Hours
Arthur Rimbaud, Illuminations*
  A Season in Hell and The Drunken Boat*
Guillermo Rosales, The Halfway House
Evelio Rosero, The Armies
Fran Ross, Oreo
Joseph Roth, The Emperor's Tomb
  The Hotel Years

Raymond Roussel, Locus Solus
Ihara Saikaku, The Life of an Amorous Woman
Nathalie Sarraute, Tropisms
Jean-Paul Sartre, Nausea
  The Wall
Delmore Schwartz
  In Dreams Begin Responsibilities
Hasan Shah, The Dancing Girl
W. G. Sebald, The Emigrants
  The Rings of Saturn
  Vertigo
Stevie Smith, Best Poems
Gary Snyder, Turtle Island
Muriel Spark, The Driver's Seat
  The Girls of Slender Means
  Memento Mori
Reiner Stach, Is That Kafka?
Antonio Tabucchi, Pereira Maintains
Junichiro Tanizaki, A Cat, a Man & Two Women
Yoko Tawada, The Emissary
  Memoirs of a Polar Bear
Dylan Thomas, A Child's Christmas in Wales
  Collected Poems
Uwe Timm, The Invention of Curried Sausage
Tomas Tranströmer
  The Great Enigma: New Collected Poems
Leonid Tsypkin, Summer in Baden-Baden
Tu Fu, Selected Poems
Frederic Tuten, The Adventures of Mao
Regina Ullmann, The Country Road
Paul Valéry, Selected Writings
Enrique Vila-Matas, Bartleby & Co.
  Vampire in Love
Elio Vittorini, Conversations in Sicily
Rosmarie Waldrop, Gap Gardening
Robert Walser, The Assistant
  Microscripts
  The Tanners
Eliot Weinberger, The Ghosts of Birds
Nathanael West, The Day of the Locust
  Miss Lonelyhearts
Tennessee Williams, Cat on a Hot Tin Roof
  The Glass Menagerie
  A Streetcar Named Desire
William Carlos Williams, Selected Poems
  Spring and All
Mushtaq Ahmed Yousufi, Mirages of the Mind
Louis Zukofsky, "A"
  Anew

*BILINGUAL EDITION

For a complete listing, request a free catalog from New Directions, 80 8th Avenue, New York, NY 10011 or visit us online at ndbooks.com